# Slec

by Stephanie Richardson
illustrated by Liisa Chauncy Guida

HOUGHTON MIFFLIN HARCOURT
School Publishers



Printed in China

ISBN-13: 978-0-547-02695-4
ISBN-10: 0-547-02695-1

4 5 6 7 8 0940 18 17 16 15 14 13 12 11 10

My dog pulls me
up the hill.

We sled down the hill.

My dog pulls my sister up the hill.

We sled down the hill.

My dog pulls my friend
up the hill.

We sled down the hill.

My dog pulls my brother up the hill.

We pull my dog
up the hill.

We sled down the hill.

# Responding

## TARGET SKILL Story Structure

Who is this story about? Where does it happen? What happens in the story? Make a chart.

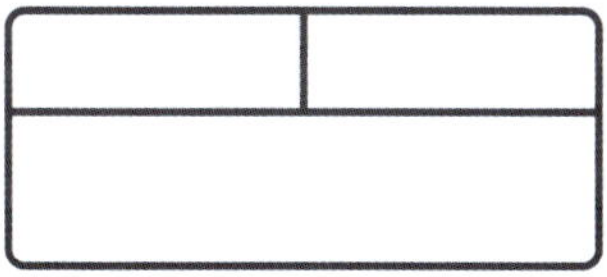

## Talk About It

**Text to Self** How else can you have fun with a dog?

## WORDS TO KNOW

| | |
|---|---|
| friend | hold |
| full | many |
| good | pulls |

**TARGET SKILL** **Story Structure**

Tell the setting, character, and events in a story.

**TARGET STRATEGY** **Analyze/Evaluate**

Tell how you feel about the text, and why.

**GENRE** A **fantasy** is a story that could not happen in real life.